Every Little Sound

**ONE
WEEK LOAN**

**FINES:
10P PER DA
IF OVERDUE**

821.92 ROB
(OWL)

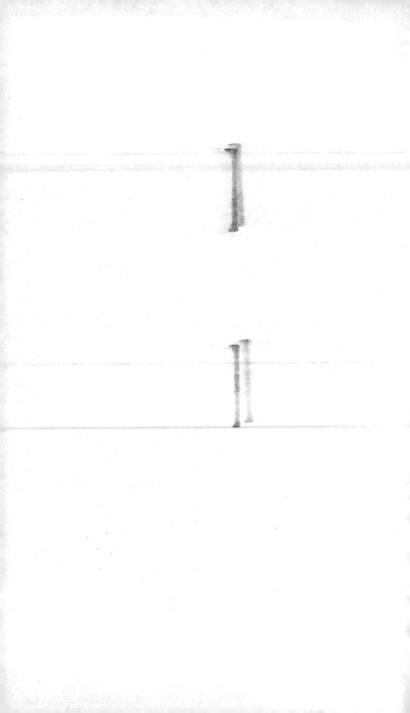

Every Little Sound

Ruby Robinson

First published 2016 by
Liverpool University Press
4 Cambridge Street
Liverpool
L69 7ZU

British Library Cataloguing-in-Publication data
A British Library CIP record is available

ISBN 978-1-78138-291-2 softback

Typeset by Carnegie Book Production, Lancaster
Printed and bound in Poland by BookFactory.co.uk

Internal gain –

an internal volume control which helps us
amplify and focus upon quiet sounds in times
of threat, danger or intense concentration

David Baguley

I've found butterflies that have literally one
wing completely gone, and they can fly.

Thomas Eisner

Contents

Reader, listener,

come in. I'm opening my door to you – the trap
door of a modern barn conversion with lots of little rooms,
vast paintings on the bare brick walls, a daring colour scheme,
sofas and awkward plastic chairs for interrogating guests

in that looking way. There's soup. Bread in the oven to warm.
Take off your shoes. Take some spare socks – I know your own feet
offend you. I know your deepest thread, like a baked-in hair.
You wish someone would think of you, spontaneously

in the middle of the night; call you out of the dark like a comet
landing on your duvet. Come in, make yourself at home.
The walls here don't have eyes. They're dumb surfaces
onto which shadows of stags are cast like stalking giants.

Unlocatable

What are you looking at? My tooth?
I pulled it out myself. I closed the door
and while no-one was watching
    (so I may or may not have existed)
I dismembered myself, dissembled
an entire vocabulary and constellations
of thoughts, disembowelled my body,

    placed my head on a shelf,
picked through everything else
with a very thin blade, like a crow on a hard shoulder
delicately inspecting the entrails
    of a mythical creature.

All my body was crying, tears
drum-rolled off my skin, which existed
    and didn't exist, like a thought
you forgot you had, like an unlocatable itch.
There was fire and fantastic smashing of chandeliers, sirens
    and the petrified calls of wild animals.

There was dust in everyone's eyes
although no-one was there to actually see
    me disintegrate, the life side-
stepping the body, askance on the bed,
a soaked towel around my sawn-off head
on the shelf, a loose thread
    holding various parts together,

tenuously. My mother, somewhere,
like a drowned fish on the very end of some
    fucker's very long line
smashing herself against the floor
to an unnatural beat, no hands to hold anyone,
    body encased in scales.

And what use am I,
half-witted, unpicked, flaked
out, half a leg, a spewing mouth, brittle hair,
    scooped-out heart crazed on the floor,
wracked with side effects?

Longbefore

She'd buried the placenta under the baby plum tree. The grass was up to her waist now and the tree's limbs laboured with purple. They said she had two weeks to clear out. The plot was unworkable. There were sixty on the waiting list. She'd stopped noticing hedge sparrows years ago but now they swathed from the hawthorn hedge to the ground and back like lapping seawater. She'd had six months to sort it out. Cut the hedges, turn over the ground, plant some things. The thing is.

She'd been busy. She used to come here before. She'd come in Tom's overalls and bring a flask of tea. The sex they'd had! In the shed, on the earthed-up potato bed, in the long grass where they'd wanted to plant the orchard. They'd been happy. They had smiled non-stop for years until.

Underneath the ripe tree, she was a young woman moulding a figure out of clay. She pushed her fingers between the legs. Longbefore, she'd been a child in a garage, potting on, picking cherry tomatoes, pickling, sucking him off. It rained for many years and she forgot about things growing. Then came Tom and his careful hands. He could thread a needle one-handed. He knew a quiet place where she'd be able to breathe. She supposed the time was now.

There was space in the garden at home for a baby plum. The sparrows faded into the hedge. She put the clay figure in her pocket so she could handle the gate's padlock with both hands.

They'd need to mend that, whoever.

Hope

It was February. Snow
wouldn't settle and things weren't beginning
anymore. Bluebottles had taken to window ledges.

On the fairway: branches of trees, driftwood, tide wrack,
one IKEA bag like a dead bird whose wings won't die

and the heart from a mammal, afloat; the lungs it was once
    moored to
thousands of miles apart; New Zealand, Jupiter.

The word *thanks*, rolling along the inside of your skull
like a marble in a bowl, a wagtail –
shocked to be on London Road: rush hour, snow storm

and notice a fragment of kebab, trodden into the kerb.
A yacht and a woman or a man, contact lenses, clothes,
anecdotes, books, cutlery, overboard. A search party

in the lobe of brain where a mother leaving the room
resides with rational thought, beige jelly
in the shape of a rabbit on a bright table cloth.

Undress

There is an ash tree behind this house. You
can see it from our bedroom window.
If you stare at it for long enough, you'll see
it drop a leaf. Stare at it now, you said,
and notice the moment a leaf strips away
from its branch, giving a twirl. Consider this.

The ash tree unclothes itself Octoberly.
From beside our bed, fingering the curtain,
observe the dark candles at the top of
that tree, naked and alert, tending to the breeze.
A sheet of ice between the rooftops
and this noiseless sky has turned the air

inside out. Black veins of branches
shake against the blue screen on which they
hang. Small mammals are hibernating
in pellets of warm air under ground. But,
in spite of the cold, this ash tree does not shy
from shrugging off its coat, sloping its nude

shoulders to the night. So, you said, undo,
unbutton, unclasp, slowly remove. Let down your
hair, breathe out. Stand stark in this room until
we remember how not to feel the chill.
Stand at the window, lift your arms right up
like a tree. Yes – like that. Watch leaves drop.

Ire

He did not show it by the way he inserted
the knife into the hot apple and split

it on the flat wood with a bang; the way he
pushed the iron pole they used to stoke the fire

deep inside the spitting twigs, the twisted news
print, timber beams, white dust. Instead,

he withdrew from her before the height
of it and he lifted a finger to the window,

to the inclement glove about their house,
flapping to come in. He peeled the duvet away

slowly, drawing heat from the flesh
just as you'd freeze-dry meat or fresh fruit.

Listen

I

Beside a sleeping child
whose womb aches, I wonder
how I know this? I wonder – can she smell me?
Does she feel the warmth
from my body? I keep expecting
to see a crescent moon
whereupon I will hang my coat, rest

a short while. I daren't speak my mind.
The man comes. I don't
speak my mind. Wiping
my abdomen, I hold tight
the sleeping child,
her dull scent, her rising ache.

II

In most homes, even the most oppressive, there are
no bars on the windows, no barbed wire fences

– Judith Lewis Herman

Sitting free, feel the certainty
of this wooden bench, the blue sky, the orange balloon
attached by string to a child's wrist.

Remember falling through a cloud,
an engine of wind at your face, ransacking your sinuses,
the cold blast peeling your eyelids back
       and yet –

a space in the ribcage
where fear should have been, or adrenalin, your placid heart
shrugging *so what?* Remember how it is to press

a keen blade to skin
and feel nothing, to go along with administering a young
mouth to rigid flesh, saying nothing.   To be truly alone,

like the man lost in Arctic snow
who, having lain down his head for a moment, to sleep
amidst the storm, never wakes up.

III

Thus, I unscrew my head,
the lid of a pickle jar.

Suspicious-looking head-
board, bed-post, -spread.

Ten thousand flower-heads
keeping themselves down.

Story

A cow walked up to a barefoot woman and licked the top of her head with its long pink tongue. Then a tall man said something and tilted his head back and his mouth grew into a huge hole that shook his skinny body with laughter. The man thought the bits of skin between his eyes and his ears would wear out and disappear with laughing. He was thankful for this. In that moment he knew that the colour green was the answer to the question that had snagged in his head since he was a small child. The woman beneath the cow started putting her feet into her boots. There was something about the warmth and smoothness inside the boots that allowed her to imagine sitting down for three days in a row on one spot, unmoving. They were standing on a big green square that was a field. That's better, something thought. The cow emptied its bowels.

Along from there, and a path next to a pond. A man caught a fly in his mouth as he was running along and he swallowed it. Two mallards on the pond were fighting. One of them was pinching the other's head under the water with its beak. A woman wearing a blue woollen hat and muddy trainers stood at the edge and leaned right over. She shouted something and kinked her bent arm towards the ducks. A stone hit the one that was on top, right on the top of its dark green billiard ball head. It snapped its bill open and shut, open and shut and it skittered across the surface of the water on untidy wings, jolting and shaking its head so that the feathers on the back of its neck became ruffled. He saw light and swathes of water and something's eye and a loud thing happening around him. The woman put her hand in front of her mouth. She rushed the side of her tongue against the sharp chip on one of her teeth back and forth. She didn't notice herself doing this in the darkness of her mouth. She didn't remove her hand from her mouth for a long time and she could feel eyes on her all over her back and shoulders. She said sorry. In the space of one blink she thought of something falling toward a hard grey floor. Then she forgot she had thought this. Her hands were out in front of her like the hands of a statue, reaching.

The running man's face was serious and empty as he ran past. The top of his head was dark pink and glistened like the skin of someone's lips. His fists were two red balls, charging at his sides. The fly was just entering the running man's stomach as he passed three women pushing three pushchairs. The moment he passed the women, the man felt a feeling that was similar to the dampened thud of a heavy door closing. He passed and it brightened. A bird was echoing its cry off the surface of some water. It became quieter and quieter. The man's body felt less heavy and the ground became very close and real. Some trees understood him and the sun pushed against his shoulders lightly.

The women, in long thin coats, were pushing the chairs in an arrow formation while maintaining a steady conversation. They had the effect of making the spring breeze seem to be inside-out. Their lips and cheeks were mobile as though they were chewing and swallowing the air ahead of them and eating up the path that the running man had left behind. The woman on the left, behind a purple pushchair, was a puppet with strings sewn tight through all her limbs, pulled rigid. She had pollen-red hair and a flat face with huge eyes and thin lips painted on. She wished she could eat a giant white baguette and hide in a tunnel of sunlight and feel her skin getting hot. She enjoyed the feel of digging her fingernails into the foam on the handles of the pushchair. She enjoyed knowing that nobody would notice her doing this. She carried on talking and mouthing the air with her head tilted back slightly so the sun slashed across her forehead. The three women didn't look over to the woman in the blue hat, on tiptoes at the edge of the pond, who wasn't quite crying.

The path next to the pond swept the running man into a wooded valley which had vast planes of green stitched onto the edges and was held up as though by poles. A boy on a red bicycle was just about to fall off his bicycle when the running man ran past. The man ran past. The boy's knee became as red as his bicycle. The boy and his bicycle made a bright stain on the patchwork blanket of fields.

Two lapwings over Mitchell's Field were throwing wide cartwheels, the sky behind them, in front of them and between them brimming with the sort of emptiness that can't be seen from the ground. Two horses with pink blankets on their backs and with long brown eyes were standing perfectly still behind a thin wire stapled to wooden staves. A collie pressed a long stick to the ground with its strong black and white jaw and swayed its rear from side to side, slowly. There was a man wearing a flat tweed cap. He was whistling for his dog and he was wondering why it is that if he doesn't drink a cup of tea in one go, he forgets about it and leaves it to go cold. He was not quite thinking about the day his wife was thrown from her horse.

On over Higger and there are several children in orange helmets rushing around, lunging from boulder to boulder. They are giant beetles hobbling over giant grey pebbles. There is a lot of sunlight and it lifts everything into a photograph-brown colour. One of the children had found a ladybird on his bed last week, at that stage near to death where the wings don't close properly, they don't work. He should have thrown the ladybird out of the window but he didn't. He doesn't know why. In between his shoulders feels tight and tickly but he can't scratch there. The ladybird's wings alarmed him. He could hear the faint scratch of them trying to move. They reminded him of his mother's crystal vase that he must not touch. He thinks of this now and can't work out why he feels a sort of ache in his fingertips. He licks the roof of his mouth, which has dried out. He jumps down from a rock and runs.

Hundreds of years ago a tiny pebble had blown about on top of a boulder and made a tiny dent in the rock. It rained and the water swished about in the dent and made it bigger and the pebble rattled and skidded around for years and years, wearing the gritstone until a big scoop was worn. This happened lots of times to lots of boulders. The children's teacher is pointing with a gloved finger to boulders with big bowls scooped out of them. Then the finger points up, up.

A curlew thrills the sky into a long ringing sound that lingers even after it has quietened. The sound is to someone a dark pink lily, gadding its head in a clean glass. The sky to the east has chilled to grey. It is the colour of grey eyes. Looking at this grey sky is like looking at someone's grey eyes, watching.

Truth

She found her mother's voice behind the sofa,
in pieces, a layer between a cup and saucer,
a trace of it in the dressing-up drawer, a sliver

between sheets of music in a box beneath
the Blüthner. She gathered it up and handed it around,
despite hugeness of cushions and swathes of rug.

Despite very tall men and women peering down,
she shared this small voice. She found echoes of it
in the resolute voices of the tall men and women,

in Radio 4 broadcasts, on tabloid front pages,
in the gleam in a celebrity's eyes, in her aunts
and uncles, in the death of a violinist, in psalms.

With it she found tiny hairs from her arms and legs
dropped off, found a brain wilted in its skull, her skin
unstuck, like petal flesh lost to a sudden hoar frost.

Locked Doors

There's a porthole in your bedroom door, the window's bolted,
cigarettes in a locked drawer, meals on a chart. You ask
permission for a cup of tea; the kitchen's locked. You ask for PRN.
You ask permission for a bath. You get your cash through a hatch

every other day. Your mind is not your own; leave a thought
lying around and before you know it, someone's inhabited it.
Someone's stealing the make-up off your face.
They've stolen your hips. In the safe, there's a bottle of vodka

with your name on it. You know beyond these doors
the atmosphere is less dense; people run on solid surfaces,
go into banks, buses, cross rivers, cut down trees. Alone
on their doorstep somewhere, someone's cutting their own hair,

noticing the warmth of a star, 93 million miles away, touching
their bare skin. All these locked doors, these eyes inside your mind,
doing the rounds. Even this plastic beaker beside your bed
is unreal, with lights out and nobody checking. No wonder

your body parts have left you. No wonder you dropped your voice
through a crack in the floor of this dim room you're locked in.

My Mother

She said the cornflake cake made her day,
she said a man cannot be blamed for being
unfaithful: his heart is not in tune with his
extremities and it's just the way his body
chemistry is. She said all sorts of things.

We saw a duck pond and a man with a tub
of maggots and a tub of sweetcorn, we saw
the walled garden and the old-fashioned library
in the park, stopped for a cup of tea in a café
where we had the cornflake cake cut into halves

with the handle of a plastic fork. We saw yellow
crocuses growing in a ring around a naked tree,
the sky showing in purple triangles between
the branches. We looked in the window
of Butterworth's at the bikes: they were beautiful

all of them. Gorgeous, she said. The sun was
pushing through the iced air and landing on us,
on our heads and our shoulders and the backs
of our legs. We bought nail varnish remover
from Wilko's, a bath sheet and two Diet Cokes.

She said she'd been talking to Jesus and God
because she didn't want to go to hell, although,
she said, correctly, we've been through hell
already, haven't we. She said a woman should
know her place, should wait. She lit a cigarette.

Apology

I can't go up because I don't know how.
Nobody has shown me.

So many names, my mother, I'm never sure
   what to call you. So many names for all your predators
   and crushes and suitors. I'm sorry.

I'm sorry I'm here and I'm sorry I'm not here.
   Would you have made it on your own
   without the comorbid condition of motherhood
   and the slowness and consistency of time?

I'm sorry for the slowness and consistency of time;
   years like zombies dawdling toward a cliff edge
   holding back the child's writhing body, itching to grow, packed
   around the same mind I have now.

I'm sorry the concept of promise outgrew the concept of child
   and that systemic contradiction and wizardry left only a dim
   sense of suspicion; a crescending breeze, accumulating clouds
   amidst bewildering dichotomies.

I'm sorry for resembling your relatives and captors and the man
   who penetrated you, who's still there, communicating boldly
   via intersections of others' thought waves and memories,
   blatant into the long nights, haunting,

   for my inferiority in the face of nuclear family culture,
   feeding on detritus of white goods, leisure sports, laminate floors,
   a real home and fake recycling,

   for creeping by night into a tight void, blinds down, brain blown
   glass-thin, electric impulses and bloated thoughts bolted in.
   For this life being the only one my quiet mind knows,

its many versions and phases, I'm sorry. I wasn't your daughter
– or anyone – when you were the blue-water navy,
or the beheaded, or the baby boy. Or was I?

I'm sorry I was not yet born and could not yet hear you
when you were over there, listening carefully
for the rain and small movements of animals, for sounds
of life, through a green, five-fingered haze.

I'm sorry I consider sentiment, fact; authenticity, originality,
when they are irrelevant. So many choices
in supermarkets, the natural habitat of panic attacks,
it's enough to make anyone sorry and I am.

I'm sorry it's taking over half a century to link your purple-patched
brain scan to the basic biology of stress. The piano thunders on,
sustain pedal wired to the facial muscles of all your neglecters,
aching like hell behind their stamina and machinery.

I'm sorry I had, logically, to think of my own self first / simultaneously,
navigating through the fire and acid of Trust and her sycophant
Love before returning. All the powerful were women; the power
of penises and facial hair originated there, cajoled by matriarchs.

As if skin and breath were insignificant! I'm so sorry.
Where are you now, to take into my arms and resuscitate?
Is it too late, given you're fifty and no longer a child?

It's always mothers and mind control which is why
I thank you for breaking the cycle, withstanding the enormity
of generations, magnetic as water, to let us go. You weren't to know

about other outrageous families and sadistic counterparts.
A nugget of my limbic system remembered choosing my own
lemon-yellow baby clothes so thank you.

I squeezed that into the thumb-sized space
in the palm of my hand knowing all along they were wrong
and imploding with it.

I'm sorry I wept in the shower for your cancelled wedding,
    letting the violet dress down the plughole, unsure
    what it all meant except things staying the same, *future*
    aggravating my brain, a baby brother gone again.

I'm sorry you were out there, alone, defined by the worst
    of others and defined by your children's prisms of hope
    and survival mechanisms. In one version, you did marry and lived
    in a house with green walls and extravagant furniture.

I'm sorry that consensus reality had you set fire to your bed
    as you lay in it; arrested, put in a cell, let off the next day
    because the lawyer believed it was a genuine attempt
    and convinced the police.

I'm sorry you've had to withstand such torrents
    of knowledgeless advice and legal toxification,
    clinging to reality by a sinew of tooth, remembering yourself,
    through the rough and the smooth.

I'm sorry I was absent, memorising books of the Bible
    for a bar of Dairy Milk, owning up to things
    I'd never done, getting confirmed as an antidote
    to the evil core of me.

I'm sorry it was exotic to think of kids like me
    ending up in prison, coincidentally, inevitably
    or prevented (which is the same), salvaged, peristalsised
    through society, brain safely contained,

    doused daily in cold water or electricity
    or disgrace, temptations kept consistently far enough away
    as to appear illusory

    like you, my brave mother, fantastic prodigy
    in flowing white kaftan, knotted long brown hair, a beautiful gaze
    of solemnity, rare stone, emotionless (defined by others).

I'm sorry I was ill-prepared for your soiled mattress
  and comatose body, under a wave of advocaat
  and transistor radios oozing with cheap Scotch. Even I
  developed feelings for them amidst adults acting like it's okay

to leave you this way, the bluebottles in on it,
  inflated with dog shit and red hot egos, resting on your cheek,
  your lip, too cunning to get rid of.

I'm sorry that laughing off a difficult childhood
  didn't make it never happen. Even a basic calculator
  recognises an infinite loop as a malfunction; don't they see *cutting*
  off my privates every night needs additional information?

I'm sorry I talked you out of wounding yourself
  although I know it feels hopeful and lets in sunlight and air
  through an open door. I'm sorry I can't help you go up.
  I, also, don't know how.

I'm sorry I prioritise the stimulation of adrenalin and opioids
  in my own axis before I come to you. Thank you
  for believing I love you even though you know
  I don't know love or trust it.

I dreamed a baby died from kidney failure. The worst part?
  Not knowing distress from relief in the face of the mother,
  like a child in an experiment. What does this mean?

My man fearing a moment of madness. Not locking the
  knives away but keeping a steady eye on them, paying attention
  to the moon and turning moods. He underestimates me;

I'm my own doppelgänger. Here I am, locked to him, discussing
  sex positions and holiday destinations. Here I am
  courting solitude in the doorway, a pair of eyes and a chest cavity

thrumming on the dark boundary between survival and self-control.
While there are no babies, I carry on. I am testament to the
   problem
of the baby. Look at me – flaunting my own survival. Who am I?

Except the parasite that accidentally caught on
to your womb wall as you lay stoned on a fur-lined coat
in a hallway in Moss Side? *Happy accident, accidentally on purpose.*

Close the piano lid. Empty a drawer. Things happen.

I'm sorry for absences, holidaying in France, studying guilt,
   time-travelling the pain barrier, intent on nerve endings
   and their connections to various biological systems.
   Learning to accept and relinquish responsibility appropriately.

Throwing back the hot stone in a horizontal line.

Thank you to the policeman who took all the men whose safety
   you feared for to the pub so you could come home
   for dinner, monologue, nail-varnish remover, a set
   of impartial weighing scales and cheap French wine.

I'm sorry about the home, the wine, the monologue resonating
   against the plastic mug others might keep for you, fussing
   over make-up-smeared walls, upholstery and understatements.
   I'm a bit sad we can't see Al. He comes on the radio sometimes.

I'm sorry I'm not bringing you home, finally, to thrive and repair.
   I wanted to stay, singing Luther Vandross on the walkway
   outside at 6 a.m., fetching toast from the neighbour. I was hoping
   for perfection, *believing in anything*, all those years.

Is it too ambitious to hope? I'm sentimentally sorry
   despite a genuine fear of sentimentality and pseudo-unhappiness,
   struggling under the weight of an A1 poster on complex trauma

and a pair of Sennheiser headphones to lock me in.
Think of what it is when God himself puts his arms around you
and says "welcome home." There's nothing mysterious

about my thoughts or affect, nor yours, nor anyone's, biologically
generated by the relationships we hide our consciousness from.
Oh unhappiness and infidelity! Disguised in metaphor

you're nothing but the deep yearning of an infant for its mother
and the furiousness. Making this connection is like remembering
being born, which is like folding time, which is no one to blame and
all the world to blame.

Thank you for picking up the handless, footless doll
  in the park, saving him from a dog or fox or thoughtless children,
  keeping him to your breast on the tram, the bus, in pubs
  and not noticing the scathing looks.

  I learnt to trust without you, leaving my thoughts
  outside for five minutes and trusting the neighbour's cat
  not to urinate on them.

I'm sorry my stand-in mother was an evil replica, machine-like
  yet unpredictable. We tried to calculate an algorithm for her
  mood, as you would've done, and in 14 years never cracked it.
  She remained seated when I left for the last time.

You weren't to know
  and they wouldn't have believed you anyway.
  We learn to accept the clouds for what they are
and wait, patiently.

Interlude

During the interlude, nothing is found or figured out. Minds unhitch
orbit-less. Eyes forget to blink. Plastic spoons, Häagen-Dazs, lipstick,
urinals, red curtains, left and right brain hemispheres are floating

in the gap between one universe and another, between a platform
and a train. A streetlight falters, an oak tree sheds its season in one
    breath,
black T-shirts reposition the world, clothed bodies descend,

pinned in place by tubes of searchlight. You hear somebody
refolding their legs, the squeak of a shoe's leather, a boiled sweet
rolling from one cheek to the other and it feels like – were the actors

to drop dead (from an after-party in the theatre bar last night,
that someone spiked) and soldiers, politicians, vicars, presidents,
the actors' mothers, sisters, brothers, the actors' fathers to burst in,

sprint past the blocks of seats, beat the corpses, rape them, set dogs
on them – judges and juries would look on through gleaming faces
as we look on now for fifteen minutes, breathing out, breathing in.

Years pass. Some shout their pain from a soundproof box
until, startled by the score from the pit, the light peeled back,
a triangle struck, we see ourselves rise from the stage and play on.

Tea

Somehow you led me home and told me again
of the Emperor Shennong's cup of warm spring water
under a tree of falling leaves. The way some leaves
fell in, browning the water. In Namche Bazaar

we held a bowl in both hands and curled the yak
butter fat and condensed milk about our tongues
as the oily smoke curled about the blackened kettle,
hanging battered, spout like a duck's beak,

above the fire. Today, in our kitchen, a person
pours and speaks, instead of you, of flavanoides,
amino acids, vitamins, polysaccharides, three minute
brewing time, a clean spoon, a hot cup.

At base camp, bed tea was brought to the tent
at sunrise. You were laughing as you recalled
symptoms of dehydration: headache, dry mouth,
dizziness on standing. Lack of tears when crying.

Time

Against a stethoscope,
even the hum of a rodent's heart
can be divided into its constituent beats
and the gaps between.

Considering this,
we bought a camera, set it on a timer,
shot our life for sixteen seconds, printed
ten thousand frames

on photo paper,
pasted them to the bedroom wall.
We put the camera on the fridge to cool, split a Cobra
into two stemmed glasses

and searched
so near to the wall we could taste
the air clinging to it, feel our breath condense,
in each shot

my wrists
locked behind your neck, the same bottle
of sambuca on the coffee table,
the door slightly ajar –

each frame
identical to the last, as one heartbeat,
displaced inaudibly,
by the next.

Romance

I'd just won again at Peanuts and we were sharing a Proper Job
on St Agnes' beach, watching the surfers with envy. *You're more
romantic than I am, aren't you?* I said. A spaniel was ecstatic

in the sea spray, following its lolloping tongue. *What –
more romantic than a stone*, he said. I thought about it. I am

in touch with my feelings. It gets that way after many years
of listening to wild confusion – you finally realise *what* music,
you half dream about babies, confident in the steadfastness

of the other half of your brain, dallying a tumbler of amber
in one hand, maintaining one eye on the movements of others.

We remained silent until the horizon enflamed the shallows
and the surfers emerged one by one. I could tell he felt like crying
and I didn't mind. We finished our beer, shook hands, went home.

Boy

Your word
balanced on the rim
of my ear   I love

to think of you
my love   those fingers
unwrapping a Galaxy

Ripple
at some lights
in the Highlands

gorse popping
pelting rain   a long
story about a grub

the size of a Murray Mint
in some woman's neck
in Kenya   watercress

straight out of the River
Stour   a makeshift raft
the time you smashed

your mountain bike
into your dad's Triumph
the time your mum and dad

sat still together
on the sofa before
they called it a day   spoke

of your grandfathers: craftsmen
one metal   one wooden
universes between them

those Coca-Cola eyes
behind the living room door   lips ajar
a word between your teeth.

This Night

This October night I am more in love
with picking tomatoes from the vine
in the greenhouse, by head-torch,
giving the beam to each bauble in turn,
spotlighting the deepest red
and, careful not to burst the skin,
tending gently to the pulling away,

more in love with taking the time
to hear the brash shriek of a young fox,
to wonder about that sanitary bin, lodged
between the trunk and branch of an oak
beside the Kirkstone road,
three full weeks after the flood,

more in love tonight, with ideas
and arbitrary things,
than I am with you. The moon is crazy,
tapping on this glass roof,
this fragile skull. The night is long.

Orgasm

A foot, like a very accurate sketch of a foot,
a sculpture, cast, poured and set
against the edge of the duvet
the rest of the body aflame,
except for two glazed eyes, observing it.

Schism

Un-demanded, entering existence. Bloody
horizon / half a peach. Tailwind uphill headwind
down. X = Y. Wing-dust of moth on Velux blind.

Block the view; spite your/self. Gust of feathers.
Dry gin. A ceiling shadow, cast against inertia
/ flickering. Consciousness exiled from the body

of a child supine on a bathroom floor, stiff,
part-formed eyes open, mouth filled in.

Watching TV

There was talk of burnt eyeballs and
sulphur dioxide that made it hard

to breathe. Livestock suffering blindness
and burning to their skin, the collapse

of the food-chain. Mutated spores. Whatever
that means. We were inside your sofa,

a box of After Eights and the Laphroaig
at our finger ends. The threads at the edge

of your rug were falling apart. I noticed
with one eye, as the other scanned

the room for the remote, an image on TV
of ashes and bones washing into the sea.

Internal Gain

One ear on the Conversation downstairs,
the other catching
echoes of planets slowly creaking
in their dark celestial closets,

a leopard was upon me warmly on my bed,
breathing as any human would.

My room was vibrating with electricity sockets
and light beams
and I could hear every little sound
my mouth made.

Outside my window
a butterfly, miniscule on a roof tile
rubbed its wings together
excruciatingly.

Breathe Deep

Even trees have mouths; miniature holes
on the backs of their leaves. Under a lens

they are the breathing-holes of whales,
cut out, washed green and spread

onto a ridged landscape of veins. And,
just as the ribcage of the soft human body

on a high mountain summit more rapidly
fastens and unfastens about the lungs,

the capillaries flushed wide, the mouth
hanging open in air tight as water, so you see

on the leaf of a tree a scattering
of tiny holes, or more – a full, deep breath.

Hush

Gate hinge
becoming.

Fallen thud.
Hand bell

clatter. School
yard. Muse.

Absolution.
Hushed auditorium.

Water swished
into an ear

around the brain
and out.

A zipper undoing
you.

Vascular circle.
Dark pump.

Door click
shut, squelch.

Hand repeating.
And over.

Five chime horn
of a train

over its rattling
track, quick

air, over your
exoskeleton,

sirens galore.

Purple, yellow,
red, marbles,

tulip heads.
Gather yourself,

belongings.
Get up, drop

into a well
lumps of sound

you cowl from.
Leave them

for another
generation,

some other child
to find.

Love

Eventually, the nerve impulse is carried
to the apex of the heart
causing ventricles to contract,
and blood to rush
to and from this muscle the size
of your fist, an engine of flesh,

the marksman's target for a bullet.
You said, *listen to your heart*
placed a stethoscope
to my jumping skin, paused.

Cleopatra compared
it to the stroke of death,
this harbouring in the heart
of an uncertain beat.

Winter

the tortoise in the fridge through the winter. V
hopping from the corner shop on the way hor
, as and when we need it. We dry our washing
We pick chillies from the medusa chilli pla
chen windowsill. We listen to the same CD over
days, weeks at a time. We eat chilli most nigh
it in turns to wash up. We talk a fair b
curtains closed. We talk about your ex-lovers. W
out chelonian hibernation and substrates. W
es talk about sphagnum moss. We check th
although we don't really know what it is we ai
. You put an extra blanket on our bed. We slee

Love II

It's not about love. Being in or out of it. How can I say? I respect you.
There are things you've done I'd never have thought of. But I'm not made
for skin sensations or the light of a candle. My natural opioids run high,
I've insects in my peripheral vision. Or have I? *Love* was said too many
hundreds of millions of times even for a strong man like you
to counteract /

      the money spider's edging closer. It traverses my open book
      as if my skin weren't skin at all, but nerve endings in exile.

Flashback

Who's to say they're *not* rummaging around inside her,
stretching her private parts while she's on the phone to me
and they're at home watching play-backs of Countdown
on VHS? Say they ignored it 40 years ago, never owned up?

(Listen to the girl who said *get your hands off my backside*
live on Radio 1. Listen to her parents' nervous laughter,
the patting of laps. It's in the archive.)

But a newspaper cutting, in a file in a locked drawer
in the woman's parents' house, of the woman rescued
from throwing herself from the twelfth floor proves it.
She's making it up; her imagination's gone riot.

The moon is gallivanting around, performing audacities
like looking at her and looking at them and not saying
with whom the guilt lies. He keeps her on a line like a fish
against a rip current and with every pull the split widens

and in they climb, peeling back her hair, scalp, skull,
the skin of her brain, settling down, listening in.
She's not the woman she would've been, they say. *I know*
I say. *You don't know her*, they say. *I know*, I say.

But I *do* know this: the half-life of a child strung
to the ceiling by her voice box, body dumb on the floor,
someone aiming something like a gun at her, telling her
it's ok, telling her she's crazy

                     to imagine such a thing.

How to Cat

Were you here now, across this t
on the terrace, rolling gravel into
of your feet, your spine stretched
this chair, I'd watch you watch m
and, like this, we'd pass time back

remembering Cape Cornwall's pebl
swollen Murray mints, giant plums
the colour of speckled eggs, a cream
licked smooth and one the shape of
we lobbed back and forth across the

the tide crept in, until we found it's ⌐
to love too much; to forget how to lo
as your fingers might forget how to ca
wildly raking the air, feeling the splash
of shallow water on skin growing num

We keep
buy our
from wo
radiators
on the k
over for
We tal
with th
talk a
sometin
tortoise
checkir

Past

When I said chequered
I didn't mean Alice in Wonderland
wandering on a massive chess board
mounting plastic horses, shooting up
        with the other pawns
        beside a black-lacquered castle.
        I didn't mean bars and grates
        snatches of sunlight and third rate
exam papers or clouds of time
like an accidental watermark on the
'story of my life'
I didn't mean guilt or anything
        to be guilty about. I didn't mean
        an unhinged head, secrets and dark eyes
        black eyes, shoplifting, addiction, assault
        or any other crime. I don't know why I said it –
it just came out
and landed behind me like a huge cloak,
squares of light and squares
of something like a deep
        hole you fall into sometimes
        on a dark night
        on your way back from the shop
        or some bright miraculous party.

Talisker Bay

Pitched under a gleaming sun, this tent
of cobalt sky, this silt-black sand,
this smashed glass sea – our entire landscape –
is too stark to believe. In rolled-up jeans

and down jackets, flicking pebbles
into a pile, watching the moon glaze
the mountains pink, watching the tide
drag itself in, we pass a pewter flask

between us, pretend to feel the heat
on our throats, cough, slap each other's
backs, laugh and finally speak, in code:
It is possible to freeze a dead body

and dip it in liquid nitrogen, making it
so brittle that, placed on a vibration pad,
it will shatter into an organic powder,
to be dehydrated in a vacuum chamber

then put through a metal separator,
as you might sift through sand for gold.

Tuning Fork

Lifting the lid, you'd tell me:
once the fork is struck,

the initial blade of overtones
quieten to one note

composed of vibrations
undetectable by the human

eye, almost silent to the ear.
I always loved the bit

about the shattered tooth,
the thrill when you lifted

the steel close to my cheek
so that I could almost feel,

as you explained it, sound waves
from each prong of the fork

cancelling each other out.
I remember our voices, raised

against each other, amplified
by the walls of this house, recall

the function of the resonator,
as simple as a table top, to which

the handle of the fork is pressed,
or a hollow wooden box.

To My Family

Eventually you'll read me,
precisely because of what you know of me.

I'm from a block of maisonettes,
ammonia-stained, serving-hatches in the kitchens,

communal yards with poles
for stringing washing between, feral cats you take in,

a neighbour smoking a pipe all day
in his deckchair, a dealer on the corner.

You were safer here as a child than you are
coming round selling stuff, riding your bike

up the adjacent hill. I'm both the one they
let a fire extinguisher off in the face of

and the one that let it off. I double back.
You'll read me in spite of me. I'm the poem

you wish had remained unwritten
as well as wishing you'd written. I'm sick,

you'll say, because you don't know
how to unsay the things you should never

have said. I can take it – I bear uncertainties.
I learned at nine months, the world

is neither to blame nor to be trusted,
we are all little gods in our own worlds,

tearing ourselves away from unbearable closeness.
I learned to rely on a figure inside my brain

returning hope gently again, again, to the shelf
on which it resides. I'm not a real person,

I'm just words. And you have not the tenacity
to smother me, so I'll wait here, written, biding my time.

Notes and Acknowledgments

Poems from this book were first published in *And Other Poems, Antiphon, Matter 9* (Mews Press), *Poetic Republic: Poems to Talk About, Poetry, The Poetry Review* and *Snap* (Templar).

My thanks to Professor David Baguley for his generous summary of the concept 'internal gain'.

The quote from Judith Lewis Herman is from *Trauma and Recovery: From Domestic Abuse to Political Terror*, Basic Books, 1992.

'Peanuts' is a game, popular amongst children, where two players face one another holding hands and each player attempts to bend back their opponent's hands and inflict pain by straining their wrist and finger knuckles.

The poem 'Apology' includes references to: *The Book of Job* and 'Prayer Before Birth' by Louis MacNeice. It also includes quotations from 'Liberation' by Harold van Lennep.

Some of the poems in this collection include quotations from my mother, Amy Farley (formerly Jennifer Cowell), including the preface to 'Apology' and the phrase 'I could hear every little sound my mouth made' from 'Internal Gain', which gave rise to the title of the collection.

I would like to thank Amy for giving her blessing to this book, for being an inspiration and for being the least judgmental person I know.

I would also like to thank Jim Gayler, Will Robinson, Jill Croskell, Wendy Robson and Penny Philcox for their support over the years.

Thanks also to Deryn Rees-Jones and the Pavilion Poetry team for making this book with me.

And finally, thank you to Maurice Riordan for his patient encouragement.